COSMONAUT CUISINE

A Cookbook for Fun Guys That Want to be Astronauts

Copyright©2024 Joseph Frank All rights reserved.

No part of this book may be reproduced without written permission of the copyright owner, with exceptions for limited quotation for the purposes of reviews.

Author: Daniel Gossard

Mycology Consultant: Joseph Frank

DEDICATION

This book is dedicated to all of you my Gumplings. I want to thank all of you for coming on this crazy adventure with me. I wouldn't be where I am today if it weren't for all of you and I can't thank you enough. From the folks that have been with me since the beginning to those that are just joining us today, you all are the greatest group of individuals anyone could have as a friend. Thank you all and buckle up! We're going to space Gumplings!

THE AUTHOR

Cross Platform Comedian Daniel Gossard, known to most as Stoner Gump, has become well known for his elevated humor and "Broccoli" infused cooking. With over 3,000,000 followers across TikTok, Facebook, and Instagram, @StonerGump has left his mark on social media. At the same time Daniel Gossard has raised tens of thousands for various charities and fed hundreds of folks in need.

The standard being set by "Herbally Infused and Chronically Bemused," Daniel is looking to help his readers go deeper into space than ever before. If deep space exploration is not your thing, no problem! With a whole new batch of delicious "Shiitake" recipes, Daniel has included something for everyone. Sweet, or savory, strong, or subtle, if you want to train to be an Astronaut, this is the book for you!

THE MYCOLOGIST:

With over a decade of cultivation experience, Joseph Frank is passionate about sharing his love of mycology with as many people as possible. As a "Shiitake" Cultivation consultant, Joseph has worked for private individuals, and international start ups alike. Joseph also runs Mushlovemarket.com, an online store where you can purchase mycology supplies and kits to grow your own "Shiitake!"

Between 1998 and 2001, Joseph spent nearly a whole year in Interlaken, Switzerland. "Shiitake" had been decriminalized, and while living in the Alps, Joseph fell backwards into the vocation of "Recreational Trip Sitter." Joseph began leading groups of fellow tourists through the mountain hiking trails, ending every excursion with a BBQ overlooking the Swiss Alps. In all that time, leading over 400 people, not one had a bad time or regretted the journey.

TABLE OF CONTENTS

Introduction 1
Definitions 3
Lightspeed Lemon Juice 13
Hyperspace Honey 15
Sandworm Sando... 17
Celestial Chocolate Bar 19
Slip Stream Smoothies.. 21
Sauteed Spaceman "Shiitake" 23
Blaster Berry Lemonade 25
Subspace Sparkling Limeade 27
Extra Terrestrial Tea.. 29
Far Out Frosting... 31
Interstellar Ice Cream 33
Pulsar Pudding... 35
Lift Off Lemon Pie.. 37
Deep Space Salad Dressing.. 39
Spacey Salsa.. 41
Perseids Pesto 43
Lunar Lemon Pasta.. 45
Gamma Gravy 47
Captain's Log..49

INTRODUCTION

By now you folks should know the drill. It's "Shiitake" not Shiitake. Now there's many different kinds of "Shiitake." Some are white, some are brown, some are big, some are small, but in the end, they all bruise blue. Be careful where you get your "Shiitake." You are not going to find the

"Shitake" we're looking for at Wally World or your regular Supermarket. It's possible to get some of these particular "Shiitake" from a friend, but the best and safest way to get ahold of your very own "Shiitake" is to grow them yourself.

It takes some time and a little work, but nothing in life worth having is easy. Put in the time, get a kit, and grow some fresh "Shiitake" of your own. Most folks don't even know you can eat fresh "Shiitake," but it's a great way to consume these magic little beauties. And with these recipes, eating "Shiitake" will no longer be a gut wrenching experience.

The main problem with eating fresh "Shiitake" is that the chitin in the cell walls of the "Shiitake" causes stomach distress. That means a pain in the gut, and a lot of time on the commode, possibly even throwing up. The great news is when cooked, or broken down with chitinase, the chitin no longer causes any problems for your belly.

The main benefit from eating fresh "Shiitake" is that they are even more potent when they are fresh. The active ingredient in "Shiitake" is broken down by heat and water over time. In order to remove the water from "Shitake" most folks add heat. Though this is effective for dehydration, it also speeds up the breakdown of the special part of the "Shiitake" that sends folks into space.

I hope you enjoy all of these recipes as much as I do. I'll see all you Gumplings in Space!

DEFINITIONS

Chitin: A fibrous polysaccharide and one of the strongest substances on earth. Arachnids, crustaceans, and insects make their exoskeletons out of chitin. Because the cell walls of "Shiitake" are made of chitin, it's very difficult for your stomach to digest uncooked. There are some prebiotic benefits to ingesting uncooked chitin, but for most it can cause stomach distress, nausea, and other digestive issues.

Chitinase: An enzyme that aids in the breakdown and digestion of chitin. Can be found in common fruits and vegetables such as avocados, bananas, beans, chestnuts, kiwifruit, papaya, strawberries, and tomatoes. When consumed in conjunction with "Shiitake", it can help prevent issues with stomach distress and make the "Shiitake" nutritional components more bioavailable.

Intention: An aim or plan. Though it seems like a simple thing, intent is a very important part of any journey. Are you an astronaut going into space to do work and important experiments, or are you a space monkey strapped to a chair enjoying the view out the window?

Set: Short for "Mind Set," and goes right along with intention. Having the right mindset is vital when heading into any journey, long or short. Understand that what happens in your journey will depend heavily on how you feel before you get started. If you are bothered by what's going on in your life, sad, angry, afraid, be aware of that. Those feelings may be unavoidable and may come up in your journey. If you aren't prepared to deal with those emotions and feelings, it may be better to put a hold on the journey you plan.

With strong intention you can create a positive mindset for your journey. By focusing on positive feelings and thoughts you can pave the path for your happy and joyous expedition. Meditation, and a focused will to keep your mind on things that bring happiness to your life will keep those feelings and thoughts in the forefront of your mind, guiding your journey to happier places that are more fun. This is easy, and not always successful, but with practice mindful intention can help you better control the trajectory of your journey into space.

Setting: The location in which your journey will take place. The setting of your journey is just as important as your mindset. If you are uncomfortable where you are, this discomfort could alter the trajectory of your journey.

Where you feel comfortable will vary from person to person, but generally you want to find a place that makes you feel relaxed and calm. It's recommended to stay away from crowds and people who are not on the same journey. For more intense journeys you may want to have some quiet time for meditation, or have your favorite music playing in the background. For less intense journeys a fun movie, or walk through the neighborhood park is a nice setting.

Above all else, it's most important that the setting you choose for your expedition be safe. If this is your first time, or you are using more fuel to go deeper into space than you have before, make sure you are in a place that is secure and safe. You can even have a friend with you to help make important choices, should you feel they might come up. Having a good plan is a great way to feel in control of your expedition, and make sure your journey is the best it can be.

Integration: Discussion of and decoding what is seen during a journey. While hurtling through space, you are going to see many things. Some will be whimsical, some will be scary, and some will be just what you need to see. Decoding vision and ideas that have been seen on an expedition can be difficult as we are seeing things from the eye of the storm.

It can be necessary and vital to have an experienced and trusted advisor to help decipher what was seen in your journey. If you have an elder, a therapist, a counselor, or someone who gives good advice, ask them how they feel about the idea of a "journey." If that person is open to the idea, they may be able to help you decode what you see on your expedition to space.

Journaling: When going on a journey it's always a great idea to bring along a journal. Write down ideas and thoughts. Not everything that comes into your mind while on a journey is going to be important, but you will find at least one idea of value every time you go on an expedition into deep space.

If you are interested in integration, keeping a journey journal can help when trying to recall what happened, and what you saw during your journey. A written document is much more reliable than a journey-weary brain.

Micro: A journey with a small amount of "fuel." If you are looking for a way to begin your journey from Space Cadet to Astronaut, and you don't want to go too deep into space, this is the way. A micro may benefit your mood, decrease anxiety, increase neuroplasticity, and the effects can last months. It's also a great way to get used to the effects of a journey without having to commit to a Macro fueled journey.

If you want to make Micro's part of your routine, there's a few things to consider. You need to get the right amount of "fuel" and a good schedule to follow. You don't want to micro seven days a week. Your brain needs time to rest, so Micro for four days and take three days off. You can Micro on this schedule for four weeks and then take two weeks off. This will help your system reset, your brain will be reset, and the Micro will be more effective over all.

Macro: Blasting off with enough "fuel" to go into deep space. This is the journey that distinguishes the Space Cadets from Astronauts. This is where we use all the skills and knowledge that we have learned so far. Before you get started on your journey, we visualize and go over our intentions. We do this to get into the right mindset. Then, armed with a journal for thoughts and ideas, we make sure we are in the correct setting that is conducive to a safe and happy journey.

When on a Macro journey, your brain's default mode network goes down. These are the typical pathways in your brain that control how you see yourself in your memory, how you regulate emotions, and has a lot to do with your sense of self. When this goes down you are able to take a "figurative" step back and have a less emotionally connected look at your life. It makes it very easy to see answers to questions you may have about yourself and your life.

Benefits: There are a number of potential benefits that can come from taking a Journey to Space. The first and most important is that it's fun and you will have a great time. In addition to the enjoyment of the experience, the potential benefits include: increased levels of endorphins and serotonin, the disabling of the default mode network, increased neuroplasticity, neurogenesis, heightened focus, creativity, and energy.

There's a potential for decreased anxiety, stress, and social anxiety as well.

When paired with talk therapy and discussion with a trusted advisor, one of the most noteworthy potential benefits is that a journey may help with depression and trauma. When going on a journey for this purpose, it's vital to have professional help, and to not go alone, with no plan.

All these potential benefits may last from three to six months.

Risks: Not everyone is a candidate for a Journey into Space. Those diagnosed with schizophrenia, bipolar disorder, or if someone has a family history of psychosis, should probably stay on earth. SSRIs are also going to keep your feet firmly planted on earth and disqualify you from taking this kind of expedition. The brain is already flooded with serotonin so you can't go on the journey and there is potential for health issues.

When all the medical qualifications are met, it's always important to go back to Set, or your Mindset. How are you feeling? Are you experiencing depression? Are you really angry? Are you in a state of mind to go off on an expedition into space? If you don't have the right answers to these questions you could end up having a negative experience.

A Bad Expedition can be a traumatic experience, but it can also be a very helpful one. When we go on a journey, we may go places we don't like, but that doesn't mean we aren't supposed to be there. Are you mad? Well, maybe you need to see why you are really upset. If you are very sad, a journey could bring you face to face with the very cause of your sadness. You may not want to be in that place, but this is where your brain has brought you.

Experiences like this can lead to something like an "Ego Death." An experience that humbles you, and reminds you just how small you are compared to the rest of the universe. This kind of journey is extremely difficult, but is recognized by most as a character building experience.

Now, beyond all of that, say you are just a monkey strapped to a chair looking to have some fun, and you get scared by what's going on outside the window. What do you do? In the words of the Hitchhiker's Guide to the Galaxy, "DON'T PANIC!!!" Relax, find a place to sit or lay down and close your eyes. Try to focus on happy thoughts. If you practiced some intention, bring to mind the positive thoughts that you gathered before your journey.

Finally, Chocolate Milk! As part of your pre launch preparation make a batch of your favorite milk based beverage from your childhood. Do you like strawberry milk? How about an Ovaltine? Whatever it is, keep some chilling in your fridge. If you are feeling like you are steering towards a negative journey, get the milky beverage and have a drink. Reminisce on happy memories tied to the sense memory of the milk. Before you know it, you will be feeling better, and ready to get back to the cosmos!

LIGHTSPEED LEMON JUICE   Micro ★ ★ _ _ _ Macro

- 100 Grams Fresh "Shiitake"
- 200 Milliliter Fresh Lemon Juice

- Place 100g of fresh "Shiitake" in the blender. Add 200 ML of fresh squeezed lemon juice
- Blend on high until there are no more chunks larger than a grain of rice
- Place the mixture in a jar and refrigerate for 45 minutes
- Strain the mixture through two layers of thick cheesecloth and freeze the juice in 2 tablespoon servings in an ice cube tray.

If consumed immediately after straining the mixture is quite potent, and two tablespoons would generate a macro journey. It is recommended to freeze the juice immediately after straining to retain the most potency. If left unfrozen the mixture will lose potency quickly, The unfrozen mixture will bring on a micro journey, no matter how much is consumed. The more you consume, the longer the effect, with little to no increase in potency.

HYPERSPACE HONEY

Micro ★ ★ ★ ★ ★ Macro
....

- ○ 1 Clean Pint Jar With Lid or a Plastic Ice Cube Tray
- ○ 3 Grams of Dried "Shiitake" per 1 tablespoon of honey

- ○ For 1 cup of honey, you will want 48 grams of dried "Shiitake". Start by grinding the dried "Shiitake" in a blender until powdered.
- ○ To prevent powdered "Shiitake" dust from getting everywhere, add the honey to the blender and pulse until the mixture is combined.
- ○ Add the honey to a pint jar, or add approximately 1 tablespoon of honey to each slot in the ice cube tray and cover with tin foil.
- ○ Store in the freezer for up to six months

SANDWORM SANDO

Micro ★ ★ ★ ★ ★ Macro

- Your Favorite Sliced Bread
- Peanut Butter
- Marshmallow Fluff or Nutella Chocolate Spread
- 1 Banana
- 1 Tablespoon Hyperspace Honey
- Toast two slices of bread
- Spread on Hyperspace Honey, then layer on banana slices to cover the honey on the first slice.
- On the second slice, spread on peanut butter, and then your choice of Nutella or Fluff.
- Combine slices of bread and consume with a napkin nearby!

CELESTIAL CHOCOLATE BAR   Micro ★ ★ ★ ★ ★ Macro

- 4 Ounces of your favorite chocolate
- 4 Grams Dried "Shiitake"
- 1 Teaspoon Coconut Oil
- Chocolate Bar
- Mold Pyrex Bowl

- Grind the dried "Shiitake" into as fine a powder as possible.
- Melt the chocolate using either a double boiler or a microwave.
- Add the "Shiitake" powder and coconut oil to the chocolate and stir until well incorporated.
- Before the chocolate cools, add the mixture to the chocolate bar mold, and allow it to firm overnight in the refrigerator.
- The recipe can be multiplied, or adjusted for different ingredients, but make sure the number of grams of dried "Shiitake" is the same as the number of ounces of chocolate. 1 Ounce of chocolate to 1 Gram of dried "Shiitake".

SLIP STREAM SMOOTHIES   Micro ★ ★ ★ ★ ★ Macro

- ○ ½ Frozen Banana
- ○ ½ Cup Frozen Strawberries
- ○ ½ Cup Frozen Raspberries
- ○ ½ Cup Orange Sherbert
- ○ ½ Cup Pineapple Juice (Plus extra if the smoothie is too thick)
- ○ ½ Cup Ice
- ○ 7 grams of your favorite dried "Shiitake" or add 4 Tablespoons of the Light Speed Lemon Juice

This is a smoothie recipe for two people. It's important to remember that you aren't going to want to drink down three cups of liquid by yourself. So, if you are the only one drinking the smoothie, cut the recipe in ½. If you add the Lightspeed Lemon Juice, the potency will be at a 2. If you add your favorite dried "Shiitake" the smoothie will be a full Macro

SAUTEED SPACEMAN "SHIITAKE"

Micro ★ ★ ★ ★ ★ Macro

- 200 Grams Fresh "Shiitake" (Sliced)
- 2 Tablespoons Olive Oil
- 3 Tablespoons Butter
- 1 Tablespoon White Wine
- 1 Tablespoon Worcestershire Sauce
- 1 Clove of Garlic minced
- ¼ Teaspoon Garlic Powder Salt and Pepper to taste

- Add olive oil and butter to a large saucepan over medium heat, then add the sliced "Shiitake". Cook the "Shiitake" until the moisture in the "Shiitake" begins to reduce, about 2 or 3 minutes.
- Stir in minced garlic, worcestershire sauce, and garlic powder. Cook another 3 minutes on high before deglazing the pan with the white wine.
- Turn heat down to low and cook for another 5 minutes.
- The recipe makes 10 portions, and can be stored in the freezer for up to 4 months.

BLASTER BERRY LEMONADE   Micro ★ _ _ _ _ Macro

- 2 Cups Fresh Strawberries (Stems removed), Raspberries, and Blueberries
- 1 Cup Granulated Sugar
- 1 Cup Fresh Squeezed Lemon Juice
- 4 Cups Water
- 1 or 2 tablespoons of Lightspeed Lemon Juice to each glass when serving

- In a blender, combine 2 cups of berries with 1 cup granulated sugar and 1 cup of water. Blend until well mixed.
- In a large container, combine the berry mixture, 1 cup of fresh squeezed lemon juice, and the remaining 3 cups of cold water.
- Add one to two tablespoons of Light Speed Lemon Juice to each cup after pouring, and drink cold

SUBSPACE SPARKLING LIMEADE   Micro ★ _ _ _ _ Macro

- ○ 1 Cup Granulated Sugar
- ○ 1 Cups Water
- ○ 1 Cup Lime Juice
- ○ 4 Cup Sparkling Water
- ○ ½ Cup Fresh Mint Leaves
- ○ 1 or 2 tablespoons of Lightspeed Lemon Juice per glass when serving

- ○ Add Sugar and 1 Cup of water to a saucepan at medium to high heat, bringing the mixture to a boil. Boil for five minutes and then remove the simple syrup from the heat before adding half the fresh mint leaves. Stir the syrup and allow it to cool to room temperature before using.
- ○ Add the syrup to a container with 3 cups of water, lime juice, sparkling water, and the remaining mint leaves. Stir until well mixed and chill before serving

EXTRA TERRESTRIAL TEA   Micro ★ ★ ★ ★ _ Macro

- 2 Cups of fresh Strawberry, Blue Berry, and Raspberry
- 1 Cup Sugar
- 16 Grams of Dried "Shiitakes"
- 5 Cups of Water

- Add dried "Shiitake" to a blender and blend until the "Shiitake" are powdered. Add the fruit to the blender, and blend until well mixed.
- Add 4 cups of water to a medium pot over high heat. Allow water to heat to a boil while following the next steps
- Add mixture, 1 cup of water, and 1 cup of sugar to a saucepan over medium heat. Stir and allow the mixture to come to a gentle boil. Simmer for 10 minutes.
- Once the 4 cups of water have come to a boil remove from heat and stir in the fruit mixture. Cover with a lid and allow the tea to steep for 10 minutes.
- Use a coffee filter, or 2 layers of cheesecloth in a metal strainer to strain the solids from the tea.
- Serves 4. Should be served immediately, but may also be refrigerated for 2 hours to chill and served cold.

FAR OUT FROSTING

Micro ★ _ _ _ _ Macro

- ○ 4 ½ Cups Confectioner Sugar
- ○ 1 Cup Unsalted Butter (Thawed, but not melted)
- ○ 2 Tablespoons Lightspeed Lemon Juice
- ○ 2 Teaspoon Lemon Zest
- ○ 2 Tablespoons Heavy Whipping Cream
- ○ 1 Teaspoon Lemon Extract

- ○ Using an electric mixer with a whisk attachment, start by mixing the butter until there are no more lumps.
- ○ With the mixer on low, add the confectioner sugar, followed by the Lightspeed Lemon Juice, lemon zest, lemon extract, and whipping cream.
- ○ Once the ingredients have been mixed and the sugar is no longer dry, turn the speed of the mixer up to high and mix for 3 minutes. Keep refrigerated and use within 24 hours.

INTERSTELLAR ICE CREAM

Micro ★ _ _ _ _ Macro

- ◯ 1 Cup Superfine or Granulated Sugar
- ◯ 1 Cup Cream
- ◯ 1 Cup Whole Milk
- ◯ 1 Tablespoon Lemon Zest
- ◯ 4 Tablespoon Fresh Lemon Juice
- ◯ 4 Tablespoon Light Speed Lemon Juice

- ◯ Mix the superfine sugar, lemon zest, lemon juice, and Lightspeed Lemon Juice together in a large bowl.
- ◯ Mix the cream and whole milk together in a mixing cup and add to the lemon mixture slowly, stirring the whole time.
- ◯ Once the sugar and lemon mixture has been dissolved into the milk and cream, add the mixture to a 9x9 pan and cover with tinfoil.
- ◯ Allow the mixture to sit in the freezer for 2 to 3 hours, or until the edges begin to freeze, but the center is still soft. Stir the mixture, cover, and return to the freezer for at least 2 more hours.
- ◯ Makes 2 large servings

PULSAR PUDDING

Micro ★ ★ _ _ _ Macro

- 1 Cup Heavy Whipping Cream
- ⅓ Cup Granulated Sugar
- 4 Tablespoons Lightspeed Lemon Juice 1 Teaspoon Lemon Extract
- ½ Teaspoon Lemon Zest

- Add the whipping cream and sugar to a saucepan over high heat. Bring the mixture to a gentle boil, stirring the whole time. Lower the temp to medium heat and allow to bubble for 2 minutes stirring constantly.
- Add the lemon zest, extract, and Lightspeed Lemon Juice and stir until thickened, about 2 minutes of a low boil.
- The mixture should be thin and pourable when you pour through a wire mesh strainer into a high temperature safe bowl like Pyrex.
- Allow the pudding to cool for 2-4 hours. Serves 2

LIFT OFF LEMON PIE

Micro ★ _ _ _ _ Macro

- 9 Inch Premade Graham Cracker Pie Crust
- 4 Tablespoons Lemon Juice
- 1 Teaspoon Lemon Zest
- 4 Tablespoons Lightspeed Lemon Juice 8 Ounce Pack of Cream Cheese
- 14 Ounce Can of Sweetened Condensed Milk

- Using a stand mixer, beat the cream cheese until it is fluffy and contains no lumps. Add the sweetened condensed milk, and mix on low speed.
- Add the lemon juice, zest, and Lightspeed Lemon Juice. Mix on low until the filling is smooth and all the ingredients are well combined.
- Pour the filling into the pie crust and chill in the refrigerator overnight.

DEEP SPACE SALAD DRESSING Micro ★ _ _ _ _ Macro

- ○ 4 Tablespoons Lightspeed Lemon Juice
- ○ 1 Clove of Garlic finely minced
- ○ 1 Teaspoon Dijon Mustard
- ○ ½ Teaspoon Honey
- ○ 5 Tablespoons Olive Oil
- ○ Salt and Pepper to Taste

- ○ Add ingredients to a 1 pint mason jar and shake well. Makes 4 servings. Goes well with bacon, avocado, and apple

SPACEY SALSA

Micro ★ ★ _ _ _ Macro

- ○ 2 Cloves of Garlic (Skin Removed)
- ○ ⅓ Cup Red Onion
- ○ 1 Jalapeno Pepper
- ○ ¼ Cup Cilantro
- ○ ½ Teaspoon Cumin
- ○ 1 Can of Tomatoes (Diced 14.5 Oz)
- ○ 5 Teaspoons Lightspeed Lemon Juice
- ○ ½ Teaspoon Lime or Lemon Zest

- ○ Cut the stem off of the jalapeno, and remove half of the seeds or leave them in if you like your salsa really spicy.
- ○ Add everything to a blender and blend until well mixed.
- ○ Serve with chips of your choice.

PERSEIDS PESTO

Micro ★ _ _ _ _ Macro

- ○ 2 Tablespoons Lightspeed Lemon Juice
- ○ 1 Clove of Garlic
- ○ ½ Cup Toasted Pine Nuts
- ○ 2 Cups Basil Leaves
- ○ ¼ Teaspoon Sea Salt
- ○ ¼ Cup Freshly Grated Parmesan
- ○ ¼ Cup Extra Virgin Olive Oil
- ○ Pepper to Taste

- ○ In a blender add the Lightspeed Lemon Juice, garlic, pine nuts, salt and pepper. Pulse until well mixed.
- ○ Next add the Basil and with the blender on add the olive oil.
- ○ Then add the Parmesan cheese before a final 15 second pulse of the blender

LUNAR LEMON PASTA

Micro ★ _ _ _ _ Macro

- 12 Ounces of Spaghetti
- 2 Cloves of Garlic
- 2 Tablespoons of Lightspeed Lemon Juice
- Zest of 1 Lemon
- 2 Tablespoons of Fresh Parsley
- Extra Virgin Olive Oil

- Cook your pasta in salted water. "Salty like the ocean." Once the pasta is cooked to your desired tenderness, save 1 cup of the pasta water, and set the pasta aside.
- In a saucepan over medium heat, add 2-3 tablespoons of olive oil. When the oil is hot, but not smoking, add the minced garlic, parsley, lemon zest, pasta water and last of all add the Lightspeed Lemon Juice.
- Stir briefly and bring to a simmer before adding the cooked pasta. Toss the pasta until well coated. Add black pepper and parmesan to taste.

GAMMA GRAVY

Micro ★ ★ ★ ★ _ Macro
....

- ○ 100 Grams Fresh "Shiitake" Sliced
- ○ ½ Pound Sausage (Casing Removed)
- ○ 4 Tablespoons Butter
- ○ ¼ Cup All Purpose Flour
- ○ 2 Cups Milk
- ○ 1 Teaspoon Thyme
- ○ ½ Tablespoon Rosemary
- ○ Salt and Pepper to Taste

- ○ Add butter to a large saucepan over medium heat, then add the sausage and "Shiitake" to a large saucepan. Cook until the meat is browned.
- ○ Add flour, thyme, and rosemary to the pan and mix until the meat is coated and the butter is well mixed with the flour.
- ○ Lower the temp to medium/low heat. Begin mixing in the milk a ¼ cup at a time. Each time you add milk, make sure to fully mix the gravy and allow it to thicken before adding more milk. Once the gravy is a creamy desired texture, remove from heat and serve.
- ○ Makes 5 servings

CAPTAINS LOG

www.ingramcontent.com/pod-product-compliance
Lightning Source LLC
Chambersburg PA
CBHW062140160426
43191CB00014B/2338